THE COMPLETE GUIDE TO
# UNINVITED ADVICE
## ON RAISING CHILDREN

# THE COMPLETE GUIDE TO
# UNINVITED ADVICE
# ON RAISING CHILDREN

ALICE BEAVEN

HODDER &
STOUGHTON

First published in Great Britain in 2005 by Hodder and Stoughton
A division of Hodder Headline

A Hodder & Stoughton Book

4

A CIP catalogue record for this book is
available from the British Library

ISBN 0 340 89869 0

Typeset by Palimpsest Book Production Limited,
Polmont, Stirlingshire
Printed and bound in Great Britain by
Clays Ltd, St Ives plc

Hodder Headline's Policy is to use papers that are natural,
renewable and recyclable products and made from wood grown
in sustainable forests. The logging and manufacturing processes
are expected to conform to the environmental regulations
of the country of origin.

Hodder and Stoughton Ltd
A division of Hodder Headline
338 Euston Road
London NW1 3BH

*For my parents, whose own advice has, of course,*
*always been impeccable*

# ✌ PREFACE ✍

Like many parents, I have received many, many
invaluable pearls of wisdom from family, friends,
passers-by and social services about the best way
to raise my children.

Conscientiously, on each occasion I have adjusted my
child-rearing techniques accordingly. I am proud to
say that little Harry has just become the youngest
child ever to receive an ASBO and Elsie is on her
third exclusion.

After extensive research, I have gathered together
for the first time all the well-meaning but uninvited
nuggets of advice that new parents can expect to
receive. Thus you can side-step the worrying chore of
consulting expert baby books and create your very
own pick-and-mix approach to child rearing, happy in
the knowledge that at least one person out there thinks
you're doing it right.

☙

# I

## SLEEP TRAINING AND ROUTINES

# SLEEP TRAINING

'The most effective method of sleep training is to put
the baby in a room sufficiently far away from your
own that you can't hear it cry. During the fifties and
sixties, children were known to go through the night
within minutes of being treated like this.'

☙

It's Henry on the phone,
darling. He says that he's
learnt to talk and can he
please get up now.

## STRICT ROUTINES

'If you want your baby to sleep through the night
at an early age, the golden rule is to establish a firm
routine and structure his feeding patterns right from
the very start.'

☙

... and at what time do you feed from
your left breast for 25 minutes, followed
by 15 minutes from your right breast,
whilst drinking a glass of water? Come
on, come on, you know this one.

# SLEEP TRAINING: TWO OPTIONS

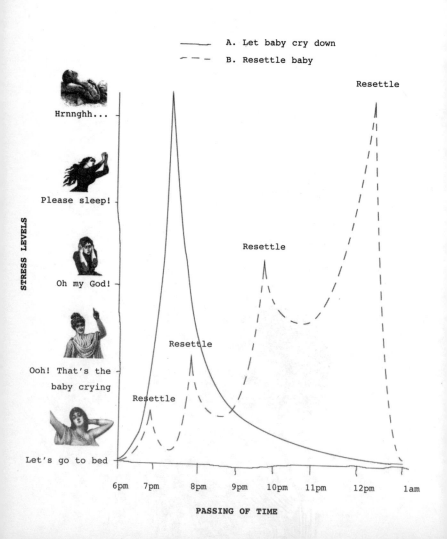

# SCHEDULE

'To force your child to sleep and feed to a schedule is unnatural.'

&

# THREE IN A BED

'It's so much easier and more natural to have your baby in bed with you and to feed on demand.'

ॐ

# PROFESSIONAL HELP

'If all else fails, why not try a sleep expert?'

'Some experts recommend that you plug in your baby monitor the wrong way round, so that he can hear you rather than you hearing him.

Their research apparently shows that it is good for your sleeping baby's development to listen to your breathing, your movements and your talk.

It is recommended that parents who are concerned about not hearing their baby cry buy an extra set of walkie-talkies.'

# II

## FEEDING YOUR CHILD

## BREAST IS BEST

'Mother's milk is the best source of all the vitamins, nutrition and immuno-protection that the baby needs.'

☙

# TODDLER EATING PATTERNS

℘

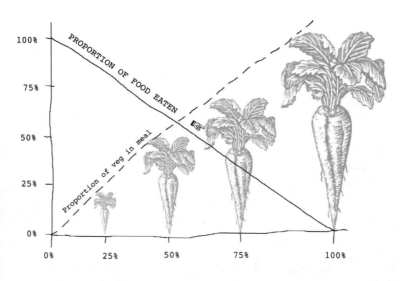

Fig 1. THE INVERSE RELATIONSHIP BETWEEN QUANTITY OF
VEGETABLES SERVED AND QUANTITY OF FOOD EATEN

15 mins preparation:    30 mins preparation:    45 mins preparation:
   75% consumption          50% consumption          25% consumption

Fig 2. INPUT OF EFFORT RELATIVE TO CONSUMPTION OF MEAL

# FOOD SCARES

'It's really important to keep up to date with the latest research on food safety.'

೫

# BREAST PUMPS

'The modern breast pump is designed to feel as
natural as breast feeding itself.'

ᴄʙ

# ALLERGIES

'How hard can it be to avoid nuts, after all?'

☙

## ADDITIVES

'If you don't expose your children to additives and pesticides at an early age, they won't develop a resistance to them.'

☙

# ASK THE EXPERTS

'For breakfast try to encourage your toddler to eat green leafy vegetables, scrambled tofu with greens, soya milk and vegetable soup.'

Crikey, this tofu tastes delicious.

Almost as good as the lettuce.

Hope there's vegetable soup and soya milk for afters.

# FADDY EATING

'If your child will not eat liver, sardines, broccoli and
ox tongue, then he is not hungry. Wait four hours and
then try again.'

# III

## HEALTH

# GERMS

'Modern mothers disinfect too much and that is why children catch colds.'

◌℘

## FRESH AIR

'Small babies love fresh air, especially if it's cold.
If left in a large pram outside on their own for an
afternoon, they always come in rosy-cheeked and
pleased to see you.'

❧

## TRADITIONAL CURES

'If your child has a cold, rub goose fat on his chest and wrap him up tight.'

'**Zedibed Cold Relief:** good for colds, fever, pain and for knocking your kids out on long airplane flights. Oh, unless they have a hyperactive reaction.'

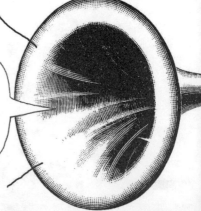

On behalf of the captain and crew, I'd like to apologise for the truly awful children in row nine.

# THE MMR DEBATE IN FULL

# CONSTIPATION

'Many children will on occasion spend a day without passing a motion, but some can hold out for over a week and this can lead to serious problems.'

☙

## IMMUNISATION

'In the First World War, children were encouraged to play 'lickety-flick' to build up their immune systems. This involved the vigorous licking of the side of an old cigarette card and their fingers before flicking the card against the kerbstone. The card closest to the kerbstone won. Of course a lot of children died, but then that's the olden days for you.'

❦

# HEALTH VISITORS

'Don't be afraid of the health visitor. They're there to help you.'

ℭℬ

# HOMŒOPATHY

'Oh, God, don't bother with doctors. Go and see a
Homœopath – they'll sort you out in no time!'

☙

'Don't worry if your child appears not to hear your instructions. Selective deafness to the female voice appears in boys at around the age of three and, sadly, only gets worse as they grow older.'

There's absolutely nothing to worry about, Mr Brown.

# BABY MASSAGE

'You really must try baby massage. It's great!'

# IV

POTTY TRAINING

## HOW TO POTTY TRAIN

'Remove your child's nappy and limit yourselves to just one room with a potty in it. Encourage your child to use the potty. Do not leave the room until potty training is completed.'

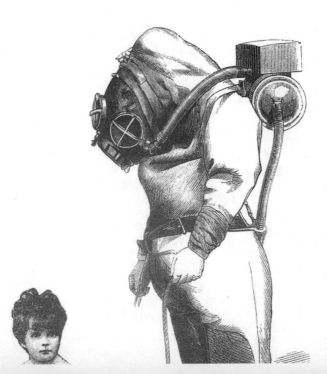

**Expert A:**

'If you try to potty train your child too young, they'll grow up to be a bedwetter.'

**Expert B:**

'If you don't potty train your child at a young age, they'll never learn to automatically control their bowels and will become incontinent in old age.'

Thank goodness for my Potty-o-matic Child Timer.

## A RADICAL SOLUTION

'Don't bother with nappies at all! Start potty training from birth. Study your child's face to learn to recognise the signals that he is about to have a movement and place him on the potty accordingly.'

THE
NO-NAPPY THEORY

As sponsored by :
DISPOSABLE SHEETS INC.

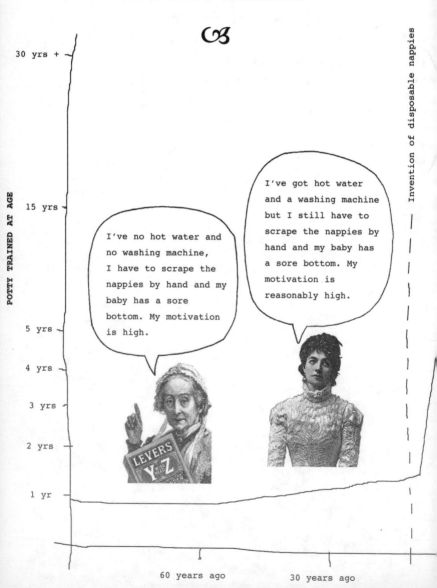

Yes, Sorry about the smell. My mother never bothered with potty training.

I've got hot water, a washing machine, tumble-dryer, disposable, odour-eating, liquid-absorbent nappies and a nanny. I'll start potty training in the summer. Maybe.

The present day                    The future

## MISSION ACCOMPLISHED

'Everything is so much easier once your child is potty trained. You can really start to get on with your life'

☙

## NAPPIES

'In the past, mothers had to to boil all the dirty nappies on the stove before preparing the evening meal for their husband.'

# V

## EQUIPMENT

## PRAMS

'All prams should be as large as possible. In the olden
days, children didn't leave the pram until puberty, so
room for growth was crucial.'

☙

## NIGHTWEAR

'All children should wear long nighties up to the age of two, irrespective of gender. Any more than one button is excessive. Poppers and zippers have only been around for the last fifty years and are clearly the work of the devil.'

ↂ

# SHIRTS

'Always to be tucked into trousers and, ideally, pants too.'

# BABY MONITORS

'If you're going to sleep well at night, you really have to get a baby monitor.'

℃

## BABY BOTTLES

'Don't waste money on baby bottles! I had an old
olive-oil bottle that I filled with sugar water, fixed a
teat on top and left it in the cot overnight. The baby
loved it! Of course, he was soaking in the morning.'

CB

## TOYS

'Ideally, children should have no toys at all.
A wooden spoon, a saucepan and some hefty
imagination is all they need to grow into
well-balanced adults.'

☙

I'm sure it's supposed to do more than this. Where's the instruction manual? Maybe it needs batteries.

# THE LIGHTWEIGHT BUGGY

'A must-have for the mum-about-town.'

**LIGHTWEIGHT BUGGY:**

Very sporty. Have been known to reach speeds of up
to 20mph in windy parks when the baby's not in them.
Often to be spotted on their backs at supermarket
checkouts when the parent has overloaded the handles
and has let go to tap in their pin number.

# THE TRADITIONAL PRAM

'The only option for those who care about their
child's posture and physical well-being.'

☙

(Do check the size of your boot. Oh, and the size
of your local shop's aisle. Oh, and...)

─── ❦ *ASK THE EXPERTS* ❧ ───

**Expert A:**

'Dummies delay the development of speech and
impede the correct development of the tongue
muscles required to speak.'

**Expert B:**

'Thumbsucking gives you buck teeth.'

# SNAP-TO BUCKLES

'As easy to use as A-B-C.'

CX

CLICK!

**INSTRUCTIONS FOR GRANDPARENTS AS FOLLOWS:**

1. Approach buckles
2. fiddle about a bit
3. Tut loudly
4. Go and get glasses
5. Try to click the wrong end of the buckle together
6. Curse to yourself
7. Pull straps out to full extent and tie them in a knot
8. Locate daughter-in-law and point out the absurdity of the design

## PLAYPENS

'Children benefit from being set clear boundaries and the easiest way to make sure your child is safe at all times is to restrict its movement.'

cs

## REINS

'I can't understand why reins have gone out of
fashion. They made it so easy to control your child.'

☙

## BE PREPARED!

'Plan your trips away with military precision. If you and your partner can work as a team, there is no reason why anything should be left behind.'

ɞ

# VI

## PERSONAL DEVELOPMENT

Yes, it's the same for me. Baby Massage, Baby Yoga, Gymbabes, Tumble Tots, Little Dippers, Tick-Tock, Gymboree, Monkey Music... I don't know where my childhood's gone.

# OVER-STIMULATION

'Boredom is good for children and encourages
concentration.'

☙

The Logi Baird family settles down for
another evening of mother's lullabies, little
suspecting the impact that lack of stimulation
would have on little Johnny.

# MAKING FRIENDS

'It's better to have a child that's a hitter than to have one that's always being hit.'

CB

# TELEVISION

'Television has a negative influence on children and encourages bad behaviour.'

&

# EXERCISE

'For their mental and physical well-being, it's important to make sure that your children get enough exercise.'

cx

## LEARNING TO SHARE

'There is nothing that gladdens a mother's heart more than to sit back and watch her children happily sharing a toy together.'

☙

## WHO DARES WINS

'Mothers these days are too protective of their
children and don't allow them to take risks.'

In Victorian times, the chance to work as a Baby Cannonball was seen as a fantastic career opportunity for the under-fives.

# THE POWER OF IMAGINATION

'Don't be afraid to explore your own inner child
when playing with your kids.'

☙

## BABY WHISPERING

'Imagine drawing a circle around your baby to delineate his personal space. Never enter this circle of respect without asking permission. Always tell him why you want to come in and what you're going to do.'

# VII

DISCIPLINE

# I BLAME THE PARENTS

'There is no such thing as a bad child, just
bad parents.'

## TERRIBLE TWOS

'If, as parents, you fail to work as a team in caring for
your child, it can lead to tantrums.'

# CORPORAL PUNISHMENT

'A quick spank is a far less tortuous and far more honest form of punishment, than the never-ending lectures you see parents giving their children today.'

'Teaching your child the skills of negotiation will equip him well for later life.'

## BAD BEHAVIOUR

'The best way to deal with bad behaviour is
to ignore it.'

♋

Madam, come quickly! The kids
have set the nursery on fire.

More tea, anyone?

# PARENTAL AUTHORITY

'Remember, you're the boss. Don't let your children undermine your authority.'

℃ß

# TIME-OUT

'Time-out can be a very effective tool in improving your child's behaviour.'

☙

## POSITIVE REINFORCEMENT

'Be sure to give your child lots of praise and positive
feedback for any extra effort they make.'

One more tug and I
reckon the whole curtain
rail will come down!

Hmmm? What? Super dear.
That's really great.
Well done.

## HOW TO REPRIMAND

'Keep your tone as calm as possible, maintain eye contact and speak slowly and clearly. You will soon find that your child will reply in kind.'

☙

'If consistently used, reward charts can work
brilliantly to communicate which behaviour is
acceptable or unacceptable.'

## TOP SHELF

'Putting the disputed object on the top shelf is the only really effective way of stopping fights over possessions.'

# VIII

# THE FATHER'S ROLE

'It's very important that the father has the opportunity to take an active role in looking after the children.'

‿

'Sibling rivalry can be avoided. Encourage your first child to feel involved with your second. Devise experiences that they can share together.'

## NEW BLOOD

'If your family has always been short, try to
marry someone over six foot. If you don't, in two
generations' time you'll all be wearing pixie hats
and sitting under toadstools.'

☙

Well, he certainly
didn't inherit it
from my side of
the family.

## BROTHERLY LOVE

'You will be suprised by how much siblings will
psychologically adjust to make room for each other.'

# DIVISION OF CHILDCARE

'There is absolutely no physiological reason to prevent men being just as good at raising children as women.'

ɞ

## PROFESSIONAL SUPPORT

'Try to make your nanny feel almost like part
of the family.'

☙

# THE MOTHER-IN-LAW'S ROLE

'Your own mother can be of great help in the early stages of childcare. Indeed, in some tribes, the grandmother will support the mother by offering supplementary breastfeeding.'

Oh, dear God, what is your mother doing now?!

# FINDING EXTRA HELP

'When interviewing nannies, it's good to have close
family with you to confirm your opinion of the
interviewee.'

☙

# GRANDPARENTS

'There is so much that a grandparent can teach a child! The knowledge that is passed between the generations is invaluable.'

☙

## GENETIC INHERITANCE

'If you peer into a pram, are suddenly confronted by an ugly baby and can't think of anything to say, enquire about family resemblance. Alternatively, admire the pram instead.'

CB

# THE FAMILY UNIT

'Don't just gawp at the telly every evening. Make time for each other! Remember, the family that plays together, stays together.'

ℭℬ

The Joneses settle down to another evening of punk classics.

# IX

## ACADEMIC AMBITION

# PRIVATE SCHOOLS

'If your child is not in private education by the age of three, academically he will be too far behind to ever get in.'

☙

# EARLY READING

'I can think of no good reason not to teach your
child to read at an early age. It opens a whole new
world of information to them.'

❧

Mother! It says here that you
have jeopardised my future mental
well-being by over-stretching me
academically at too young an age.

## SUPPORTING YOUR CHILD

'You've really got to push to make sure that the school recognises your child's full potential. Extra work at home really helps in getting your child ahead of his peers from the start.'

Dear Sir,

I would like to complain. Despite my having purchased the entire range of your 'Baby Eureka' DVDs, my child still appears to be as thick as two short planks.

# ACHIEVEMENTS

'Don't be shy about letting everyone know about your child's achievements. Other mothers in particular will love to hear about how well yours is doing.'

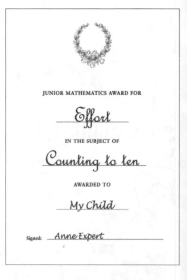

CERTIFICATE OF

# EXCELLENCE

IN THE APPLICATION OF

## *sticky paste*

PRESENTED TO

*My Child*

By: *Anne Expert*

*Third Prize*

FOR

**NOSE BLOWING**

AWARDED TO

*My Child*

Signed: *Anne Expert*

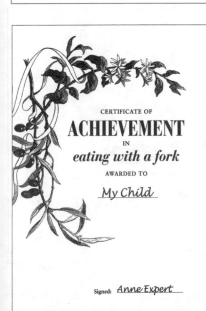

CERTIFICATE OF

# ACHIEVEMENT

IN

## *eating with a fork*

AWARDED TO

*My Child*

Signed: *Anne Expert*

AWARD FOR

**ACHIEVEMENT**

IN

**using the potty**

*Presented to*

*My Child*

Signed: *Anne Expert*

# BABY SIGN LANGUAGE

'Teaching your child to sign enables them to communicate at a much younger age than their non-signing peers.'

CB

# CHILD PRODIGIES

'If you want to unlock your child's full potential, it's
important to start at a very young age.'

An early performance by the Lloyd Webber brothers

# BABY SWIMMING CLASSES

'Young babies have an amazing natural instinct to swim which should be tapped into. Their little legs and arms will instinctively paddle through the water.'

☙

'The most valuable skill you can teach your child is the ability to focus.'

..and the capital of China is Beijing. Can I please watch telly now?

# HOW TO BE A WINNER

'To give your child confidence, make sure that
they are always top of the class. Step in and help
if necessary.'

&

# SEX EDUCATION

'Don't pass your own sexual hang-ups on to your
kids. Talk about sexuality and express yourself.'

❦

## A JOB WELL DONE

'When you think about how much advice is available
to parents today, there is no reason why we shouldn't
all be producing perfect children.'

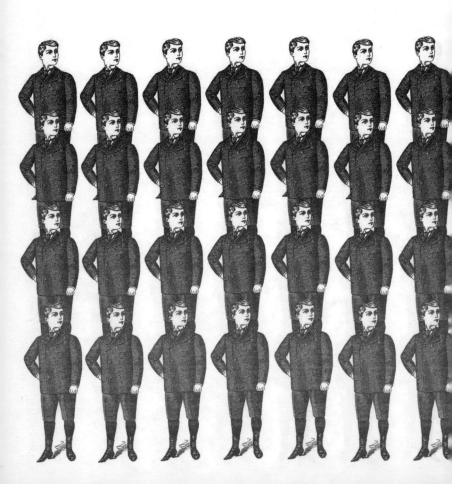

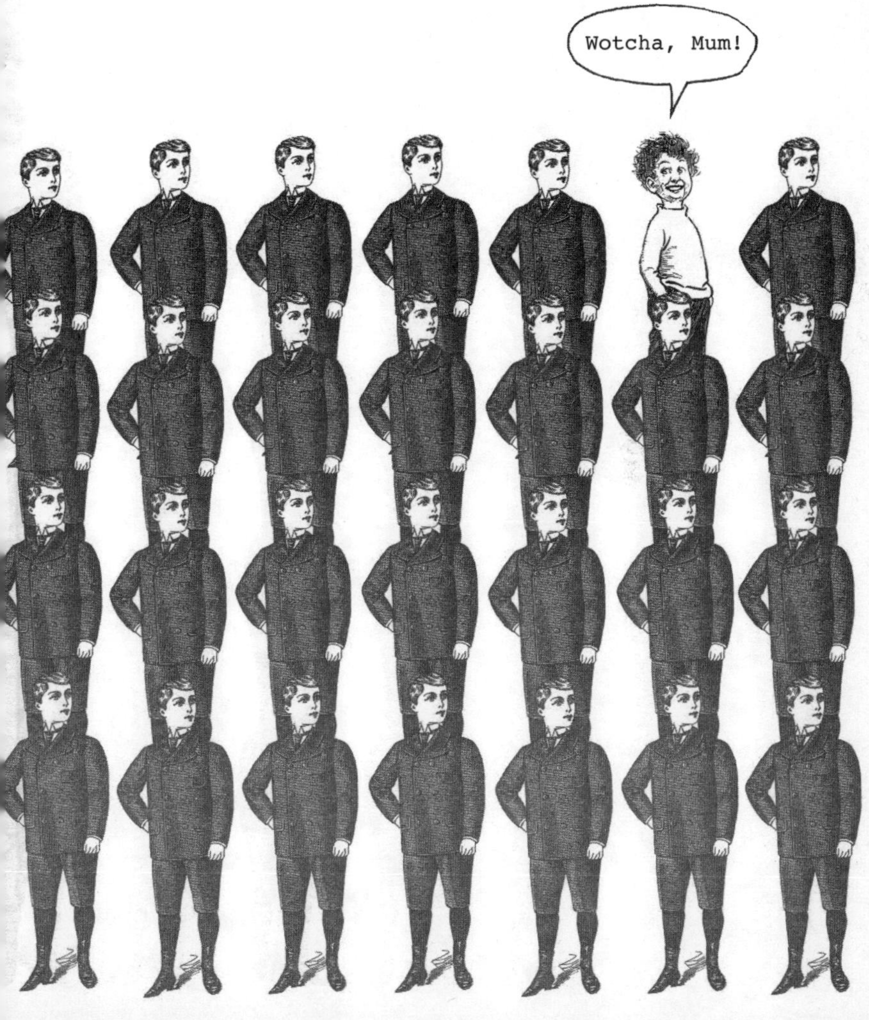
Wotcha, Mum!

.